· FUN · WITH · MATHS ·

COUNTING

LAKSHMI HEWAVISENTI

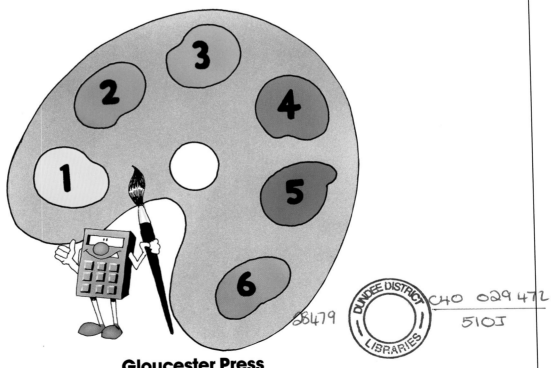

Gloucester Press
London · New York · Toronto · Sydney

© Aladdin Books Ltd 1991

All rights reserved

Created and designed by
N.W. Books
28 Percy Street
London W1P 9FF

Design: David West
Children's Book Design
Editor: Melanie Halton
Illustrators: John Kelly
Ian Moores

First published in Great Britain
in 1991 by
Franklin Watts Ltd
96 Leonard Street
London
EC2A 4RH

ISBN 0-7496-0556-1

Printed in Belgium

A CIP catalogue record for this
book is available from the British
Library.

CONTENTS

DOMINO ADDING	4
COUNTING GAME	6
CLENCHED FISTS	8
TIC-TAC-TOE	9
MAYAN JUNGLE	10
SCORING SQUARES	12
FOUR IN A LINE	14
ROCK AROUND THE CLOCK	16
HAPPY TELEPHONES	18
NUMBER GREETINGS	19
CODED PICTURE	20
PAPER CUP BOWLING	22
CARD GAME	24
CODE NAMES	26
ITALIAN CODES	27
SHOVE COIN	28
OTHER CALCULATORS	30
INDEX & ANSWERS	32

INTRODUCTION

This book is full of games and activities which will help you to add and take away more easily. You can play a memory game with cards, make your own dominoes for new games and learn a number code to read secret messages. By the time you've tried most things in this book your maths should be much better! Have fun!

DOMINO ADDING

Dominoes is a game in which you take turns to match numbers until you get rid of all your pieces. If you don't own a set of dominoes, you can make them. Then see which numbers you can make by adding the pairs.

What you need

Scissors

Card

Pencil

How to make dominoes
Cut 14 identical squares from card. Draw the numbers 1 – 6 as spots or circles, like they are on dice. Draw two lots of each number and leave two cards blank. Put two squares together to make a domino.

Try dice
If you don't want to make your own dominoes, you could try playing this game using a pair of dice. Which number is missing? Make a note of all the different totals you find.

4

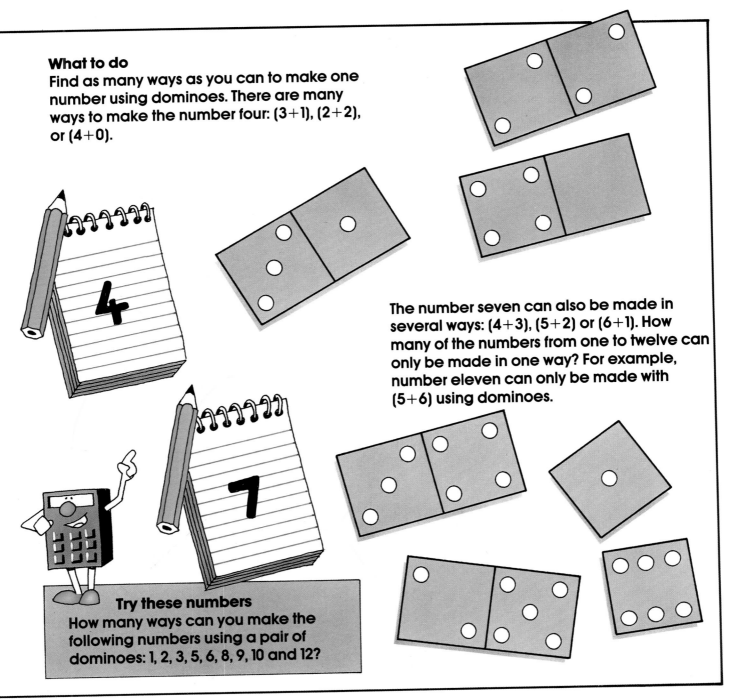

What to do
Find as many ways as you can to make one number using dominoes. There are many ways to make the number four: (3+1), (2+2), or (4+0).

The number seven can also be made in several ways: (4+3), (5+2) or (6+1). How many of the numbers from one to twelve can only be made in one way? For example, number eleven can only be made with (5+6) using dominoes.

Try these numbers
How many ways can you make the following numbers using a pair of dominoes: 1, 2, 3, 5, 6, 8, 9, 10 and 12?

5

COUNTING GAME

This game is based on darts. In darts, players throw three arrows at a numbered target and add up their points. With each turn they add their new score to their last one.

How to make it
Draw circles, one inside the other. Use a compass or two round objects of different sizes. Number the circles as in the picture and draw lines between them.

On the playground
Draw the board with chalk and use small stones or rubbers instead of coins.

Compass   Coins   **What you need**
Paper

Brush

Paint   Scissors   Pencil

What to do

Decide where to stand. Take turns to throw two coins at the circles. Add the two numbers you score and write them down. The score shown below is 9(4+5), and on the right it is 8(7+1).

Keep adding on your new score. You need 50 points to win.

Taking away

This time you start with 50 points each and play as before. Add your two numbers but this time take them away from your total. Examples: (4+5=9), (50-9=41).

Here the score is 13(8+5). Add it to the score at the top of the page and you get 8+13=21.

CLENCHED FISTS

How good are you at counting on your hands? Here you use your fingers to score. You and another player start by clenching a fist. Count to three then each make a number with your fingers.

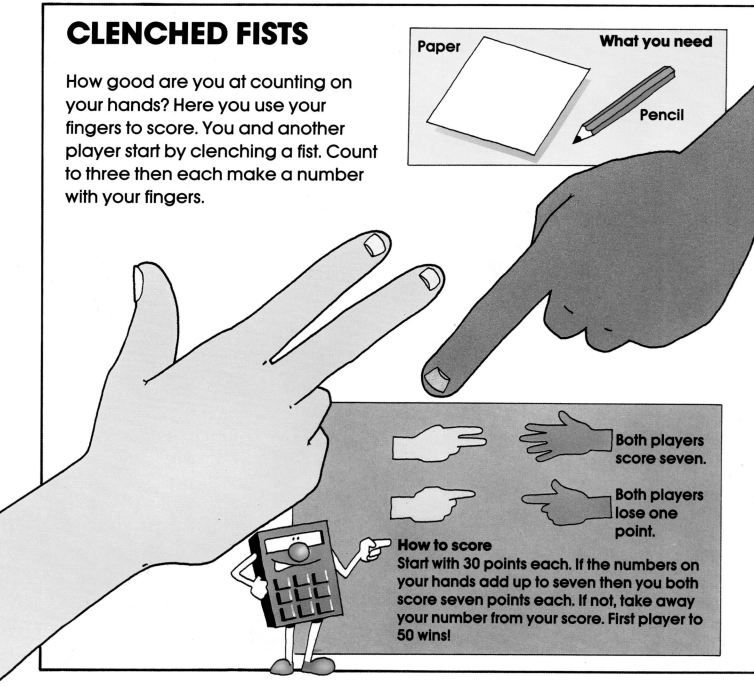

Paper

What you need

Pencil

Both players score seven.

Both players lose one point.

How to score
Start with 30 points each. If the numbers on your hands add up to seven then you both score seven points each. If not, take away your number from your score. First player to 50 wins!

TIC-TAC-TOE

This game is just like noughts and crosses. But here you try to get three cards of the same colour in a row.

How to make it
Cut five squares out of each colour of card. Number the two sets one to five.

What to do
Copy the grid. Take turns to put your cards on the squares. Make a row (up, down, across or diagonally) of three to win all the points on the board.

What you need

Pencil   Pen   Paper   2 Colours of card

9

MAYAN JUNGLE

The Mayans were an ancient tribe in Central America. They used dots and lines to write numbers. Mayan numbers will lead you through the jungle to the hidden temple.

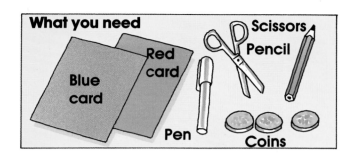

What you need

Blue card

Red card

Scissors

Pencil

Pen

Coins

How to make it
Cut out 10 red cards the same size and number them 1-10 in Mayan. Repeat for the blue cards. You can play on the picture shown opposite, or trace it.

•	1	▬	6
••	2	•• ▬	7
•••	3	••• ▬	8
••••	4	•••• ▬	9
▬	5	▬▬	10

How to play
Mix the cards in each pile. Pick a red and a blue card. Take away the numbers and move this number of steps.

7
− 3
4

How to trace
Trace image on to tracing paper.

Turn your trace over and pencil shade image.

Draw over image again.

SCORING SQUARES

How many boxes can you make? Complete the squares by joining the dots and win the points inside. The more boxes that you can finish, the more points you will score.

How to make it
Copy the grid below using lined or graph paper. The dots should form the corners of a square around each number.

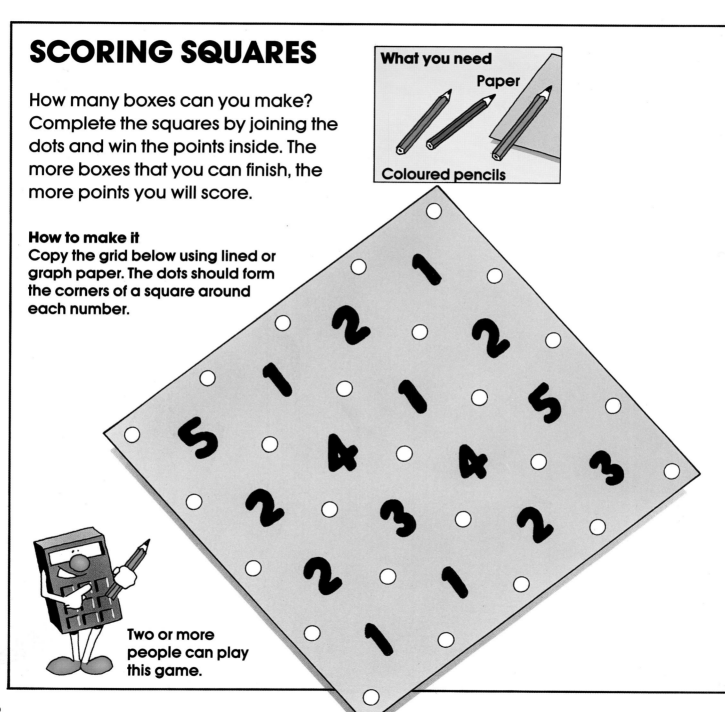

What you need

Paper

Coloured pencils

Two or more people can play this game.

How to play

The first player joins any two dots with a line (A). You must not draw over the numbers. The next player does the same (B). Take turns until all the dots are used.

How to score

When someone makes a box with a number in it (see picture D), he or she scores these points and can then have another turn. Keep a note of all the points you each score, and add up your totals at the end.

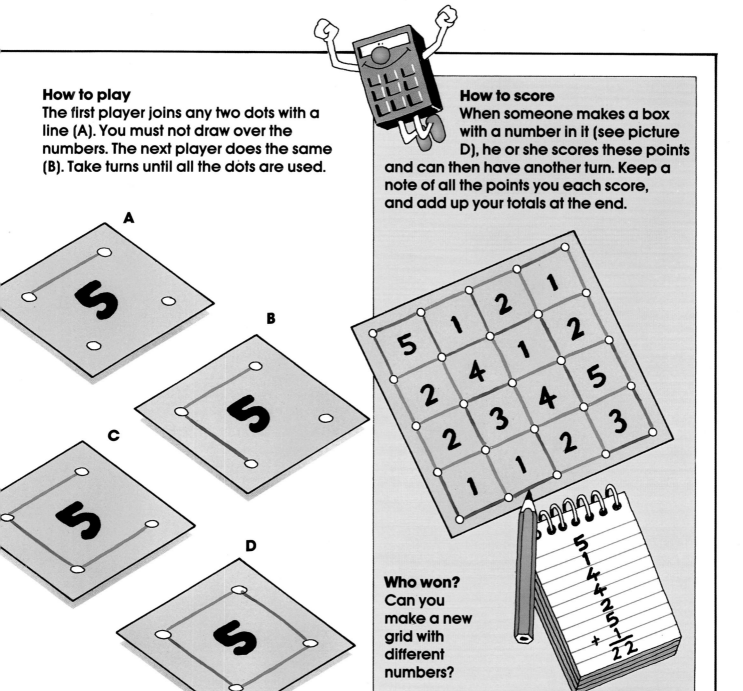

A

B

C

D

Who won? Can you make a new grid with different numbers?

13

FOUR IN A LINE

The great thing about this game is that you choose whether you add or take away. Work out the answers to the sums to see where you can put your counter.

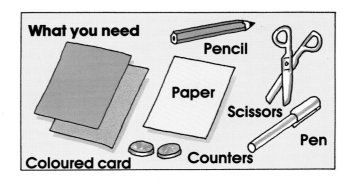

What you need

Pencil

Paper

Scissors

Pen

Coloured card

Counters

How to make it
Cut eight squares out of each colour of card. Number the two sets 0-7.

What to do
Take turns to pick a card from each pile. You can add your cards (6+4=10) or take them away (6-4=2). Put your counter on the number you get.

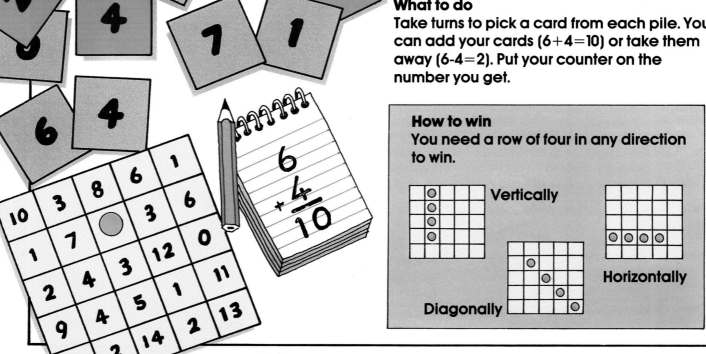

How to win
You need a row of four in any direction to win.

Vertically

Horizontally

Diagonally

14

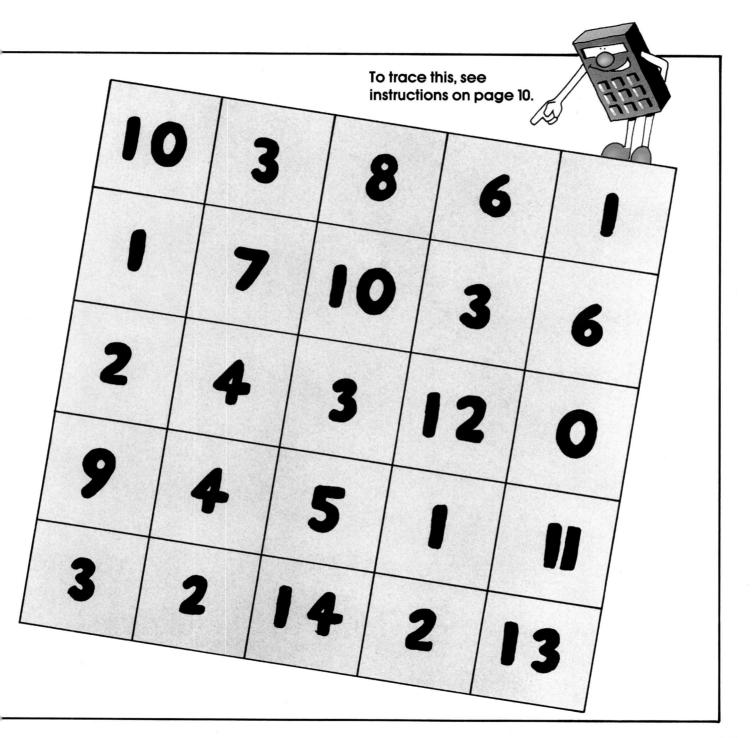

To trace this, see instructions on page 10.

ROCK AROUND THE CLOCK

Can you win in the race against time?
To find out, do some take away sums.
Beat the clock by being first to get all
three of your counters to 12. You
can use the clock opposite or trace it.

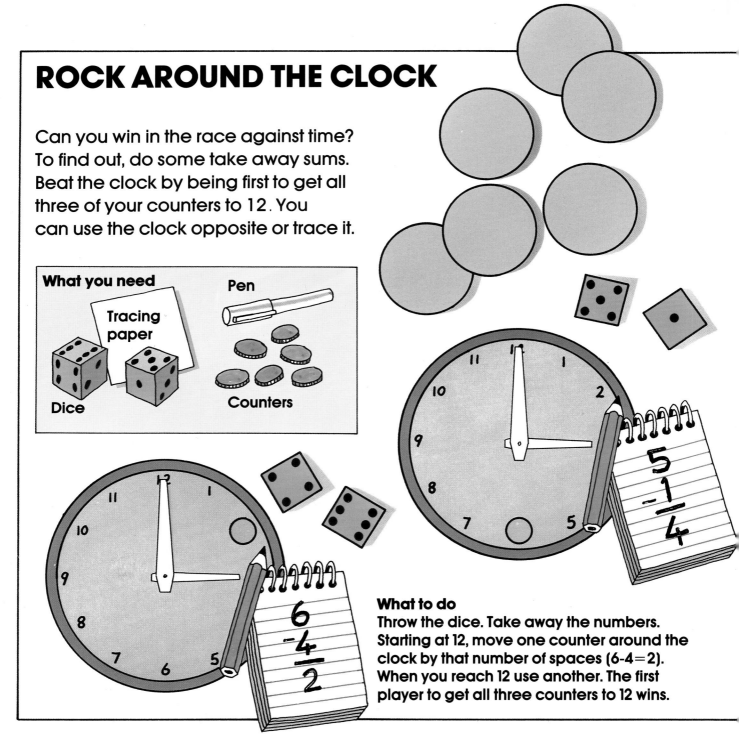

What you need

Tracing paper

Dice

Pen

Counters

$$5 - 1 = 4$$

$$6 - 4 = 2$$

What to do
Throw the dice. Take away the numbers.
Starting at 12, move one counter around the
clock by that number of spaces (6-4=2).
When you reach 12 use another. The first
player to get all three counters to 12 wins.

To trace this,
see page 10.

HAPPY TELEPHONES

How many "happy" telephones can you find? All you need is a pencil, paper and some telephone numbers. If you don't know any numbers make them up. Follow the instructions below.

What you need

Paper

Pencil

EXAMPLE
Make up a telephone number, for example, 789 2346

What to do
Choose a telephone number and add up all the digits. If you end up with more than one digit, add them again (see A and B). Keep adding until you are left with one digit (see C). If you get five, your number is happy!

NUMBER GREETINGS

Did you know that your calculator could talk to you? All you need to do is work out the take away sums below. Use a pencil and paper for these. Don't cheat and use your calculator.

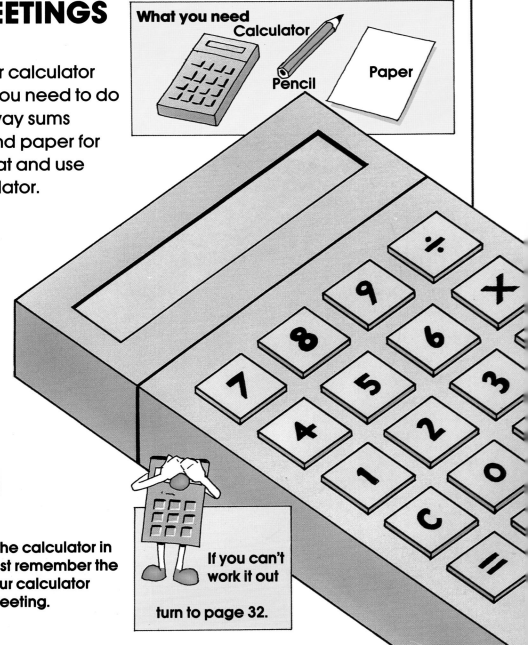

What you need
Calculator
Pencil
Paper

Try these
Work out the sums below. Do them in your head or use a pencil and paper.

A 14-14=

B 14-7=

C 10-3=

D 10-7=

E 11-7=

What to do
Now key your answers into the calculator in this order: A.B C D E. You must remember the point sign (.) after A. Turn your calculator upside down to read the greeting.

If you can't work it out

turn to page 32.

CODED PICTURE

Can you work out the code to help you paint this picture? First solve the sums. Each sum represents a colour. The answers to the sums are the numbers on the picture.

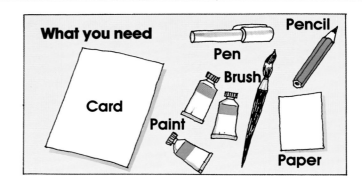

What you need

Pencil

Pen

Brush

Card

Paint

Paper

What to do
Trace the picture opposite on to card. Work out the sums below. Each one has its own colour on the palette (right). So, if the answer to question one (yellow) is 14, all the spaces numbered 14 on the picture will be painted in yellow.

Find the code
Work out the answers to these sums to see how to colour in the coded picture.

1. $7+3+4=$

2. $14-3=$

3. $25-10=$

4. $11+4-2=$

5. $2+3+9+11=$

6. $20+4-12=$

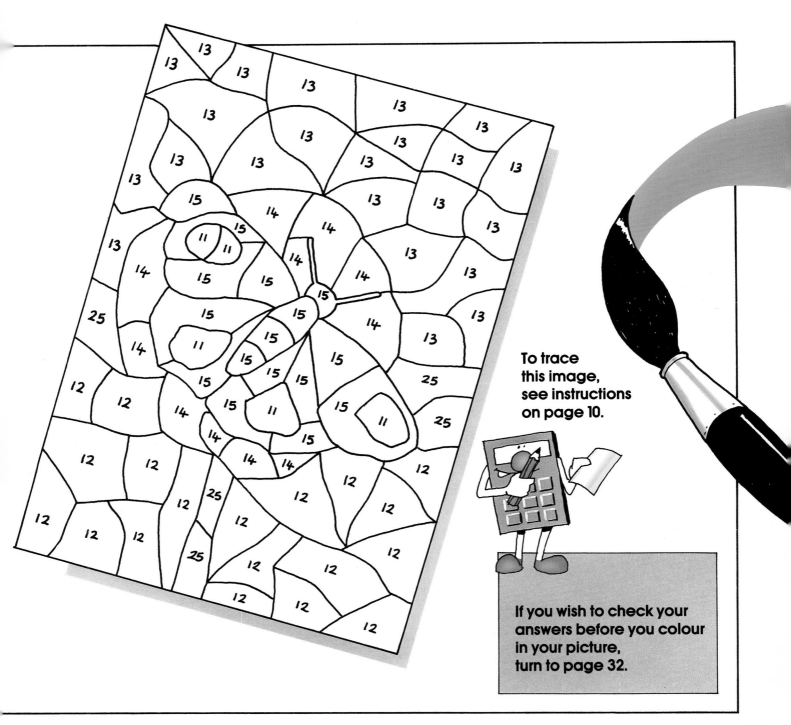

To trace
this image,
see instructions
on page 10.

If you wish to check your
answers before you colour
in your picture,
turn to page 32.

PAPER CUP BOWLING

This fun game for two or more players is based on the game of skittles. Players use a ball to knock down as many skittles as they can. Use paper cups as skittles.

What you need

Paper

Pen

Paper cups

Tennis ball

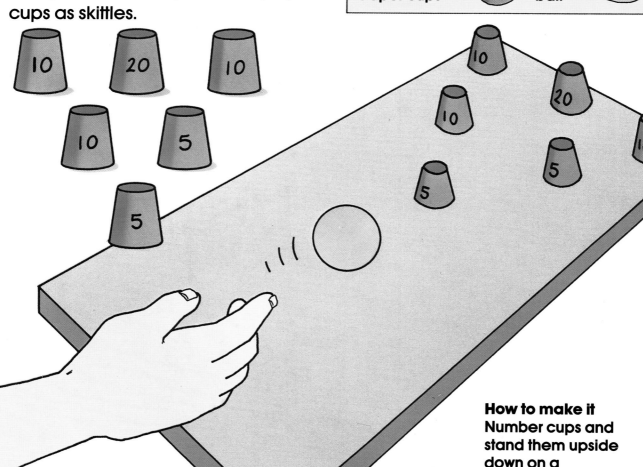

How to make it
Number cups and stand them upside down on a table, as shown.

How to play

Start with 100 points each. Take turns to roll the ball gently to knock down the cups. Add up the points on each cup that you knock over. Take this total away from 100 the first time, and from your latest total on following turns (100-35=65). The first player to use up all the points wins.

Try doing this

To change the game, why not try swinging the ball instead. The ball will have to be attached to string and tied to a frame or the bottom of a chair. Score as before.

Try another game

Add up the points. The first player to reach 100 wins.

CARD GAME

In this game you use a pack of cards. Try to find as many pairs of cards as you can that add up to ten. You will need a good memory to find the ones you want.

Preparation
Take out all the cards numbered between two and eight. Check that you have 28 cards. Shuffle them well. Lay them face down in neat rows, as shown on the opposite page.

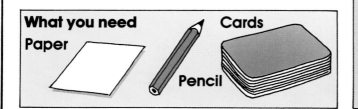

What you need
Paper
Cards
Pencil

Using a pack of cards
Whenever you play with a pack of cards, you should make sure that you mix them well before you start.

What to do

Take turns to turn over two cards. If they add up to ten (like 6+4=10) then you can keep them and have another go. If they do not, like (5+2=7), turn them face down again in the same place.

How to win

When all the cards have been used up, count up your pairs. The player with the most pairs is the winner.

CODE NAMES

What is the secret code for your name? You can use numbers instead of letters to write the names of all sorts of things. Eleanor's code is 70. What is your code?

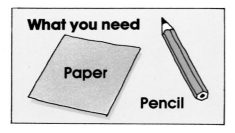

What you need

Paper

Pencil

$$5$$
$$12$$
$$5$$
$$-14$$
$$15$$
$$+18$$
$$\overline{70}$$

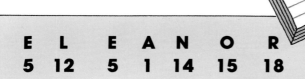

E	L	E	A	N	O	R
5	12	5	1	14	15	18

What to do
Use the chart to give each letter of your name a number. Add up the numbers to crack the code.

Which animal is this?
4   15   7   =   ?

Make some codes of your own now. You can make some for your friends too.

A	1
B	2
C	3
D	4
E	5
F	6
G	7
H	8
I	9
J	10
K	11
L	12
M	13
N	14
O	15
P	16
Q	17
R	18
S	19
T	20
U	21
V	22
W	22
X	24
Y	25
Z	26

ITALIAN CODES

What do the Italian words in the sums mean? Each word represents a number, the way the word two = 2.

What to do
Look at the sums below. Find a number to replace the Italian word that will leave the correct total for the sum. Write your answers on paper.

OTTO + 3 = 11

CINQUE + 5 = 10

DODICI − 6 = 6

QUINDICI − 6 = 9

Once you know what the numbers are, you can use the chart on the left to work out the letters that each number represents in the coded message below.

If you can't work it out, the answer is on page 32.

OTTO =

CINQUE =

DODICI =

DODICI =

QUINDICI =

SHOVE COIN

This game is usually played on a large wooden board. The board is polished so that coins slide easily along. Play with two or more players or in teams.

How to make it
Copy the grid shown on this page on to card. Put holes in the corners. Attach string to the corners of the board. Now tie the board to the legs of a table, as shown on the opposite page. Make sure the coins you use are small enough to fit on the spaces.

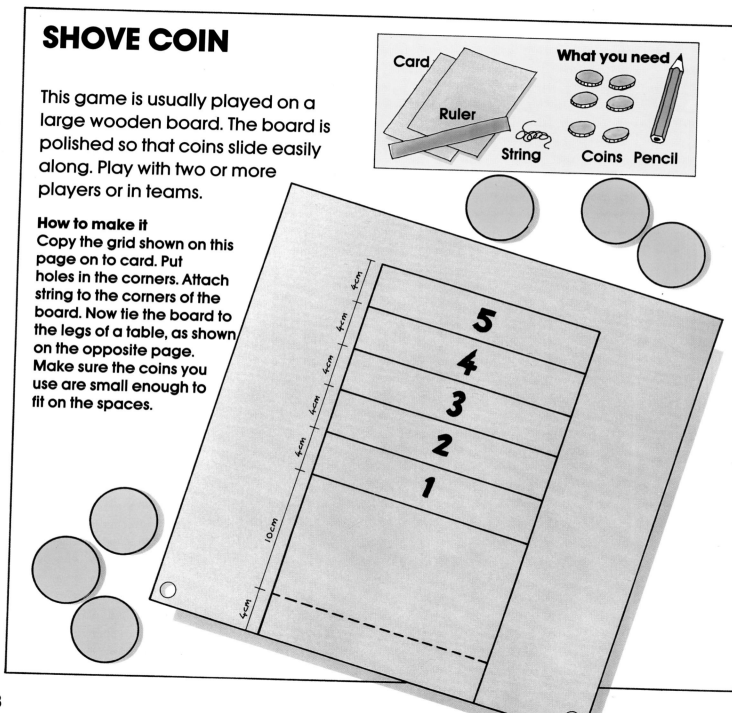

Card
Ruler
String
Coins
Pencil
What you need

5
4
3
2
1

4cm
4cm
4cm
4cm
4cm
4cm
10cm
4cm

What to do
Place your coin behind the dotted line. Using the heel of your hand, take turns to "shove" your three coins along the board. Add together the numbers you score. The first player to reach 100 wins. If you score 5+5+5, you take another turn!

5
4
+ 2
11

Circle Ball
You can try a similar game in the playground. Use chalk to draw large circles, one inside the other, on a wall. Number them one to four.

To play, kick a ball at the circles. Do this three times. Score by adding together the points for each circle you hit. The first person to score 100 points is the winner.

OTHER CALCULATORS

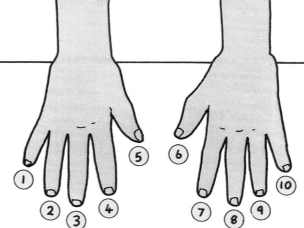

HANDS

Using your hands is the easiest way of adding and taking away for numbers up to ten. But how can we calculate bigger numbers? Here are a few ideas to try.

ANSWER THIS

1	l		
2	ll	6	ЦНТ l
3	lll	7	ЦНТ ll
4	llll	8	ЦНТ lll
5	ЦНТ	9	ЦНТ llll
		10	ЦНТ ЦНТ

ЦНТ
ll
+ lll
= _____

STICKS

Using sticks instead of numbers is a quick way of counting. Use the chart to work out different sums. Can you use the chart to find how to write other numbers? Try 15 or 12.

STONES

Stones can be used to help you add or take away. Collect 20 stones and make up some sums. Lay the stones in rows as shown in the picture. The answer to your sum should be clear.

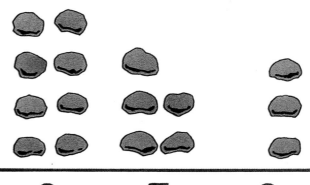

8 − 5 = 3

RULERS

Rulers can make good calculators. To answer (12-5) draw a line 12cm long (A). Now mark off 5cm (B). Next measure the other part of the line (C) to find the answer to your sum.

$12 - 5 = 7$

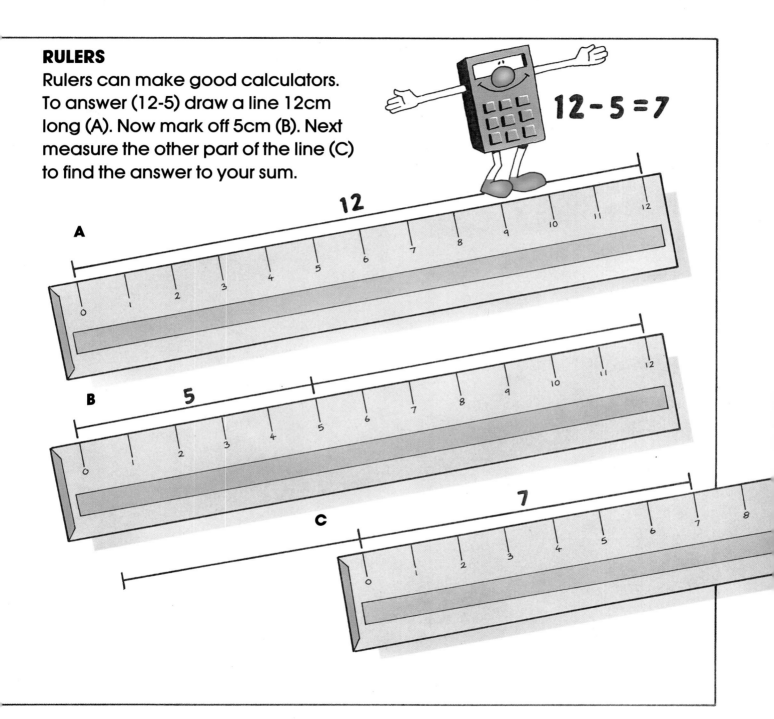

A   **12**

B   **5**

C   **7**

INDEX

calculators 19, 30, 31
card game 24, 25
circle ball 29
clenched fists 8
clock race 16, 17
code names 26
coded picture 20, 21
codes 20, 26, 27
counting game 6, 7

darts 6
dice 4

domino adding 4, 5
dominoes 4, 5

four in a line 14, 15

hands 8, 30

Italian codes 27

Mayan writing 10

noughts and crosses 9

number codes 20, 26, 27
number greeting 19
numbers, telephone 18

paper cup bowling 22, 23

rulers 31

scoring squares 12, 13
shove coin 28, 29
sticks 30
stones 30

Page 21

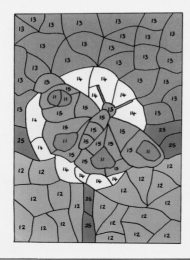

ANSWERS

Page 4: Missing number = 0

Page 5: How many numbers?
Three (1, 11, 12)

How many ways? 1(1), 2(2), 3(2), 5(3), 6(4), 8(3), 9(2), 10(2), 12(1).

Page 19: A=0, B=7, C=7, D=3, E=4 (see below)

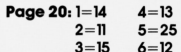

Page 20: 1=14   4=13
2=11   5=25
3=15   6=12

Page 26: Which animal? dog

Page 27: otto = 8, cinque = 5, dodici = 12, quindici = 15

Coded message: hello

Page 30: Answer this: 10

My First Time

Starting School

Kate Petty, Lisa Kopper and Jim Pipe

Aladdin/Watts

London • Sydney

© Aladdin Books Ltd 2007

Designed and produced by

Aladdin Books Ltd
2/3 Fitzroy Mews
London W1T 6DF

First published in 2007

by Franklin Watts
338 Euston Road
London NW1 3BH

Franklin Watts Australia
Level 17/207 Kent Street
Sydney NSW 2000

Franklin Watts is a division of Hachette Children's Books.

ISBN 978 0 7496 7492 2

A catalogue record for
this book is available
from the British Library.

Dewey Classification:
372

Printed in China
All rights reserved

Illustrator: Lisa Kopper

Photocredits:
All photos from istockphoto.com except 5 — Brand X.

About this book

New experiences can be scary for young children. This series will help them to understand situations they may find themselves in, by explaining in a friendly way what can happen.

This book can be used as a starting point for discussing issues. The questions in some of the boxes ask children about their own experiences.

The stories will also help children to master basic reading skills and learn new vocabulary.

It can help if you read the first sentence to children, and then encourage them to read the rest of the page or story. At the end, try looking through the book again to find where the words in the glossary are used.

Contents

4 Walking to school

6 Meeting the teacher

8 Painting time

10 Maria is crying

12 In the playground

14 Finding the bathroom

16 Working on shapes

18 Story time

20 Time to go home

22 Glossary

24 Index

Today is Sam's first day at school.
Mum and Jenny are taking him there.

Dad says goodbye at the end of the road.
"Be good, Sam, and have a nice day."

Sam sees lots of children on the way. They wave and shout to each other.

He wonders who else is starting school for the very first time today.

Some children take the bus to school.

Sam's new teacher is there to meet him.

"Hello, Sam. I'm Miss Smith.
Here's your peg. It has your name on
it with a picture of a pig underneath."

6

"Maria is new today too.
Why don't you both come along with me?"

Sam just wants to hold Mum's hand.
He feels a little strange and shy.

7

Some children are putting on their aprons.
They are going to do some painting.

"Would you like to paint something too?"
Sam pulls an apron over his head.

8

Sam is ready to start painting so
Mum says she'll leave him now.

But Jenny doesn't want to go!
Sam says he'll paint a
picture just for her.

What do you like
to draw or paint?

Sam enjoys painting his picture.

He doesn't really notice when Mum
and Jenny go to do some shopping.
They won't be gone for long.

Sam sees that Maria is crying.
He goes to find out why.

Someone has knocked over her tower of blocks.
Sam helps her build it up again.

It's time to play outside in the Sun.
One at a time on the slide!

Sam wants to go in the pedal car
but the teacher tells him to wait.

Be careful
on a slide!

12

"You must take turns," says the teacher.
"Will you let Maria go first?"

Maria has a turn, then a bell starts to ring.
They have to go back inside.

Sam wants to know where the toilets are.
Miss Smith shows him the way.

He washes and dries his hands.
Now he's ready for a drink.

14

Maria has already
finished her drink.
Sam is thirsty. He drinks very fast.

He wants to go outside again
to have his turn in the car.

A glass of milk
is good for you.

15

"The car must wait until tomorrow, Sam.
We've got some work to do now."

"I want you to find another shape
like this one. Can you do it?"

Sam hopes that he can.
"There it is. This is fun.
What else should I find?"

"Try the square and
the circle next."

An abacus helps
you to count.

Miss Smith will read them a story now,
so they must all stop talking.

Sam turns to Maria but she says, "Sssh!"
So he settles down to listen quietly.

The story is about a spider.
They sing about a spider too.

The children know some
actions for the song.
Sam finds he can soon join in.

Can you clap
and sing?

19

It's time to go home already.
Mum and Jenny are waiting for Sam.

"Where's your coat, Sam? Find your peg."
"Here it is — it's the one with the pig."

Sam sings his spider song all the way home.
He's looking forward to school tomorrow.

He'll have his ride in the pedal car
and see Maria — his new friend.

teacher

pegs

painting

blocks

22

play

working

story time

singing

23

Index

abacus 17

bathroom 14

bell 13

blocks 11, 22

bus 5

clapping 19

counting 17

drawing 9

drink 15

feeling shy 7

friends 21

goodbye 4

milk 15

outside 12

painting 8, 9, 10, 22

pedal car 12, 15

pegs 6, 20, 22

play 23

reading a story 18

shapes 16, 17

singing 19, 21, 23

slide 12

story time 23

teacher 6, 22

working 23

Find out more

Find out about your child's first day at school at:

http://www.pbs.org/parents/goingtoschool/before_school.html
http://www.pitara.com/parenting/school/preschool.asp
http://www.teachernet.gov.uk/teachingandlearning/library/firstday/
http://cbs2.com/local/local_story_215210922.html